THROUGH
A GREAT DOOR

BOB SHELTON
FOREWORD BY BOB JONES III

BJU PRESS
GREENVILLE, SOUTH CAROLINA

Library of Congress Cataloging-in-Publication Data

Shelton, Bob, 1929-

 Through a great door : missionary stories from the heart of Bob Shelton / Bob Shelton ; foreword by Bob Jones III.

 p. cm.

 Includes bibliographical references and index.

 ISBN 1-59166-355-5 (perfect bound pbk. : alk. paper)

1. Shelton, Bob, 1929- 2. Missionaries—East Asia—Biography. 3. Missionaries—United States—Biography. I. Title.

 BV3405.S54A3 2004

 266'.61'092—dc22

 2004016108

Cover and inside images provided by Bob Shelton

Map by Jim Hargis

All Scripture is quoted from the Authorized King James Version.

Through a Great Door: Missionary Stories from the Heart of Bob Shelton

Design by Micah Ellis

Composition by Melissa Matos

© 2004 BJU Press

Greenville, South Carolina 29614

Printed in the United States of America

ISBN 1-59166-355-5

15 14 13 12 11 10 9 8 7 6 5 4 3 2

TO THE GODLY MEN AND WOMEN

WHO HAVE BEEN USED OF THE LORD

TO GIVE DIRECTION TO MY LIFE AND MINISTRY

Keep looking up, Masaru

Maranatha

Bob Shelton

I Cor 15:58

I wish to express my heartfelt thanks to the faithful people of the BJU Press for their efforts in preparing and printing this book, with special thanks to Suzette Jordan for her keen insight and wise counsel.

CONTENTS

PROLOGUE   ix

1   THE CALL OF THE ORIENT   1

2   THE OPPORTUNITY OF A LIFETIME   6

3   WE CALLED HIM "BILL"   13

4   HOME AT LAST   23

5   BON VOYAGE   32

6   ARRIVAL IN VIET NAM   44

7   THE CONVICTION WAS STRONG—I MUST GO   52

8   A GREAT DOOR . . . MANY ADVERSARIES   64

9   FULL CIRCLE   72

EPILOGUE   77

FOREWORD

Glimpses of God are what the reader will find in these vignettes of missionary biography. Those who love Jesus Christ will love these manifestations of Himself through His servants Nan and Bob Shelton.

Though no man has seen God at any time (John 1:18), we know what God looks like when we look at Jesus Christ: "And the Word was made flesh, and dwelt among us, (and we beheld his glory, the glory as of the only begotten of the Father,) full of grace and truth" (John 1:14).

In addition, the invisible things of God from the creation of the world are seen and understood in what He has made, "even His eternal power and Godhead" (Romans 1:20). Man can know something about His eternal power and nature because of what is clearly seen and understood through what He has made; therefore, the Bible tells us that man is "without excuse" (Romans 1:20).

The life of Christ Jesus is also made manifest in the mortal flesh of His servants (II Corinthians 4:11). The degree to which this occurs in His servants is the measure of their worth. "Not I, but Christ" (Galatians 2:20) continues unto this present hour to be the theme of the Sheltons' life. These remembrances of their former years in foreign missionary service have the fingerprint of Christ upon them. Making Him to be seen and known is all they have ever lived for, and the record of the works of God through them—which you hold in your hands—reveals that the living Creator-God, through His servants, is still making Himself known unto men.

Bob Jones III

PROLOGUE

While other boys six or seven years of age wanted to be firemen, policemen, or cowboys, I wanted to be a preacher. It was common for me to invite my young neighborhood friends to gather on our front porch for "church." I didn't have twelve hundred people to preach to as my pastor did, but there were usually eight or ten. Of course, before I "preached," we prayed, sang, and even took an offering. The tin can that we passed never received any money, but my "congregation" was generous with their stones, marbles, buttons, and acorns. I never heard the muffled laughter of Mom and Dad as they sat unnoticed behind a door to the living room. I suspect that God was observing those services as well and perhaps with a smile on His face said again, "Suffer the little children to come unto me for of such is the kingdom of God."

A BLESSED HERITAGE

Rex and Esther Shelton

The year America's Great Depression began, 1929, something else happened that did not catch the world's attention but was important to Rex and Esther Shelton—I was born. Dad worked hard to keep food on the table for us and Mom was just as diligent to prepare that food with love and a song. One of the tenderest recollections of my childhood was Mom singing in the kitchen. She had something that I later wanted. His name was Jesus. The faithful testimonies of my parents created the hunger in my heart to know their Lord.

The seed that my parents planted was then watered in our local church with its godly undershepherd, Dr. H. H. Savage. Our church, the First Baptist Church of Pontiac, was the first Baptist church in the state of Michigan. Dr. Savage was its thirty-second pastor. Under his ministry, as a boy of five, I opened my young heart to God's crucified and resurrected Son. I trusted Christ alone as Lord and Savior. My sister and brother could later give a similar testimony of God's grace.

Dr. Savage had a vision for missions that resulted in the sending of missionaries throughout the world, but his concern for his own "Jerusalem" was just as great. He encouraged us young people to be active in the work of God. This often involved our taking part in the Sunday and midweek services. He also challenged us to witness to people on the street, in the city rescue mission, and even in the county jail. The first message I ever preached was to hardened criminals, who were waiting in our local jail to be sent to the Jackson State Penitentiary. Some of them were "in for life." As I concluded that brief message, I said, "You had better come to Christ now—you have no assurance you will be here tomorrow." One of the prisoners who knew he would be there for a long time yelled, "Give dat kid a pill."

The young people of the church were an active force for the Lord at Pontiac High School. We met each morning in the classroom of a teacher who was a member of First Baptist. Other Christians joined us as we studied God's Word and prayed together. We then faced the challenge of our studies and our encounters with classmates who needed our Lord.

Another vision that Dr. Savage shared with the church was to reach out in neighboring areas and establish branch churches. Eventually twelve branches became independent and self-supporting. Two of those churches were pastored by outstanding young men who had finished their training at Bob Jones College. One of them, Tom Malone, pastored the Marimont Baptist Church. The other, Jimmy Mercer, pastored the Memorial Baptist Church. They encouraged me to attend their alma mater. After much prayer I followed their advice and made my way to Bob Jones University. It was 1947, the school's first year in Greenville, South Carolina.

COLLEGE DAYS

From the fall of 1947 through the spring of 1951, I sat under the tutelage of some godly and capable professors. From the chapel platform I experienced the dynamic ministries of Dr. Bob Jones Sr. and Dr. Bob Jr., who desired to "keep the chapel platform hot" through preaching anointed of the Holy Spirit and the power of His Word. God also used a host of visiting conference preachers such as H. A. Ironside and Oswald J. Smith to challenge the student body. My heart began to burn for the opportunity to enter the ministry as a full-time servant of Christ. The commission from my Heavenly Commander kept ringing in my ears: "Lift up your eyes, and look on the fields; for they are white already unto harvest."

I thought I would be more effective in the ministry if I were married, but I was willing to go with or without a wife. After three and a half years, I knew I had not met God's choice for a life's partner, so I prepared to graduate without plans for marriage. God had other plans. One evening during the second semester of my senior year, my friend Cecil Lewis came charging into my room and said, "Bob, I just saw the girl you are going to marry. I met her in the yearbook office." I laughed and asked for her name. He replied, "Nancy Harrison." Actually, for some time I had been noticing a certain young lady on campus and was quite surprised when I learned later that she was the same one that my friend had met. It wasn't long before I had the opportunity to meet Nancy. I spotted her one day in line at the post office, introduced myself, and promptly made a date with her for church. Three weeks later as we were riding on the back seat of a bus on our way to her society outing, I asked her to go steady. It didn't take long until we knew the Lord had brought us together and we were making plans for marriage.

Nancy Harrison and Bob

Later, Nancy confessed that she did not realize what the Lord had in store for her when she accepted my proposal, for in the years that followed she would take on the role of missionary, pastor's helpmate, and evangelist's wife. In over fifty years of marriage never once have I heard a complaint from my faithful companion regarding location or ministry.

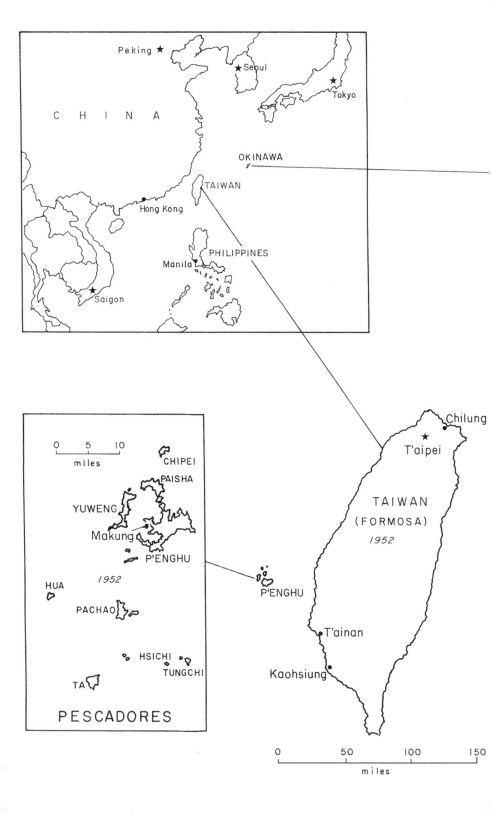

0 5 10 15
miles

KADENA
AIR BASE ▲
Naha
Yaka
1953-1955
OKINAWA

C H I N A

Mekong

Hanoi ★

L A O S

HAINAN

Mekong

THAILAND

Bangkok

Mekong

CAMBODIA

Tuy Hoa

Ban Mé
Thuot

TAN SON NHUT AIRPORT
★ Saigon

Sadec

Mekong
Delta

1957-1961

Bac Lieu

Gulf of Siam

South China Sea

0 50 100 150 200
miles

FOR A GREAT DOOR AND EFFECTUAL IS OPENED UNTO
ME, AND THERE ARE MANY ADVERSARIES.

I CORINTHIANS 16:9

CHAPTER ONE
THE CALL OF THE ORIENT

Following graduation I traveled with my college quartet. I had sung and preached with this group since my freshman year. Before the tour was over I received a call from Dr. Bob Jr. urging me to consider a challenge he had just received from Dick Hillis, a veteran missionary to China and Taiwan. Dr. Hillis hoped that BJU and other Christian colleges would respond to an invitation that had been issued by Generalissimo and Madame Chiang Kai-shek. Their desire was to recruit a team of preachers who would go to Taiwan (formerly Formosa) to preach in the Nationalist Chinese army camps.

When World War II came to an end, the Generalissimo was still in conflict with a foe from within. He had won the war with Japan, but his forces were depleted, weary, and no match for the Communist army under the leadership of Mao Tse-tung.

On October 1, 1949, Chairman Mao proclaimed China to be the People's Republic of China. By 1950 over three million Chinese had fled from China to the island of Taiwan. Among them were more than five hundred thousand Nationalist Chinese soldiers. Chiang Kai-shek planned to retreat to Taiwan for a few months of rest, to re-group, and then to return to the mainland to liberate the nation from the grip of communism. This was also the hope of the Taiwanese, for there was considerable tension between the Taiwanese and their Mandarin-speaking brothers from the mainland.

Most of the soldiers were Buddhists, so the temples in Taiwan were filled with soldiers asking Buddha to allow them to return to the mainland to liberate their beloved country. Many of them had left their wives and families behind with the promise they would soon return from Taiwan; but when 1951 arrived, they began having doubts about returning to their homeland. They believed Buddha had failed them, so these five hundred thousand men were experiencing a vacuum in their hearts that cried for help. President and Madame Chiang knew that the vacuum of the heart could be filled only by Christ. He and the Madame promised Dick Hillis that the doors to every army camp would open if God's servants came to preach the gospel.

Dick came to America to begin his recruitment program. He spoke at the Winona Lake Bible Conference in Indiana of the Generalissimo's request and the immediate need for a band of preachers who would respond to the challenge. A farmer by the name of Roger Damer and his wife, Louise, were in the Billy Sunday Tabernacle that evening and heard the challenge. They both felt the need to be involved. Roger asked the Lord to permit him to go, but the Lord seemed to whisper, "I want you to stay on the farm and do what I have called you to do, but I will bring someone into your life whom you can support." God doesn't call all of His children to preach, but He commands every Christian to be a part of His plan to get the gospel into all the world.

SPECIAL PEOPLE

Roger and Louise Damer had attended a Jack Shuler crusade in Ft. Wayne, Indiana, in 1950. Louise trusted Christ as Savior during the meetings, but Roger, under deep conviction, returned to the farm in his lost condition. Years later he wrote the following: "One night as I was taking the cows to pasture I came to the end of Roger Damer and realized I was getting nowhere. I asked the Lord to take over. . . . There was a new joy of knowing I had eternal life through nothing which I had done. . . . I just received Christ and I am now a sinner saved by grace."

Roger and Louise Damer and family

Roger and Louise grew rapidly through the Word of God and the faithful ministry of their home church. During their early walk with Christ, there were many who encouraged them to live for the Lord with a whole heart. Certain young men from Bob Jones University were among those encouragers.

With the challenge from Dick Hillis pressing on his heart, Roger felt led to write to Dr. Bob Jr. with the pledge that he would support a preacher whom the school would select to preach in the army camps of Taiwan. As the Lord would have it, the challenge from Dick Hillis that BJU send a man to Taiwan and the letter from Roger Damer promising to support such a man landed on Dr. Jones's desk in the same delivery of mail.

Dr. Bob asked his secretary to contact the office of the director of ministerial training. The secretary for the extension department was Miss Bobbie Cochran (she later married my good friend and classmate David Yearick). Bobbie responded to Dr. Bob's inquiry by saying, "I suggest we send Bob Shelton."

Dr. Bob sought the Lord's direction in prayer, then called me with a challenge that would change the course of my life. Our quartet was in the middle of the summer tour when his call came. Those on the team urged me to go. After much prayer I, too, believed it was God's will, but there were some changes I would have to consider. I then contacted Nan and was relieved to hear her say, "I believe this is the will of God. We should postpone our wedding." I rejoiced to know that God was giving me a wife who wanted Him first in everything.

Sometime later in a letter to Nan, I wrote,

> Of course, I will miss you, Honey, but for some reason I know
> that God will bring us back together next fall, and we will find
> that our love for one another and the Lord is even stronger
> than it is now—This is what the Lord meant when He told us
> to seek Him first. As Dr. Bob says, "You never find happiness
> looking for it—you stumble over it on the road of duty." I've
> seen many young people who spend all their time looking for
> happiness—how foolish. God will give us that if we continue
> to put Him first. And we will by His Grace!

In another letter I expressed similar feelings, "I find it difficult
sometimes to put first things first, but if the Lord is going to bless
us in the future, we must honor Him in the present."

I was scheduled to join Dr. Monroe Parker as his song leader as
soon as the summer tour was completed. He not only wanted me
to lead singing in his crusades but he also planned to give me a
year of "on the road" training to further prepare me for the work of
an evangelist. After much prayer, Dr. Parker released me with the
assurance of his prayer support for the Lord's special blessing on
the challenge before us in Taiwan.

CHAPTER TWO
THE OPPORTUNITY OF A LIFETIME

Several young men, fresh out of college, arrived in Taipei, Taiwan, about the same time. Dick Hillis met us and again we were challenged with the unprecedented opportunity before us. At last, the vision of Chiang Kai-shek was about to be realized. The name Dick used to identify this work was The Formosa Gospel Crusade.

I was assigned for the most part to preach in the army camps of southern Taiwan. Other teams worked in the north and central parts of the island. Gene and Dean Denler, identical twins from Illinois, were to stay with me for most of my ministry. We had much in common—we were about the same age, lovesick, and engaged to be married. Gene played the cornet and Dean the trombone. The Chinese servicemen were enchanted with identical twins who could make music such as they had never heard, and they were willing to stand for an hour or more under a tropical sun to hear the Denlers' music and the preaching of the gospel.

Army camp evangelism

The schedule was as demanding as anything we had ever experienced. Some days we had meetings in three or four army camps. From early morning until late afternoon we were shuttled from camp to camp. Since this ministry was sponsored by Chiang Kai-shek, the soldiers were required to attend. It was not uncommon to go to a camp to find three thousand, five thousand, or even ten thousand servicemen standing at attention waiting to hear the gospel story. At the end of those busy days we welcomed the sight of local Chinese hostels. They became our "homes away from home," for it was there we could shower, relax, write our letters to Nan, Mary, and Ruth, and sleep.

In a letter to Nan dated April 11, 1952, I reported, "We are still having three to five meetings a day, and 50 to 400 accept Christ in almost every service." A few days later I wrote, "The first meeting today was with the tank corps. I really didn't know what to expect, but 383 of those soldiers accepted Christ as Savior. My throat was so sore I could hardly talk because I had to shout so loud to make them hear. Gene and Dean preached at the other services. I am getting my voice back now and will start preaching again tomorrow. Continue to pray."

About six months later when all of the camps had been reached, the teams assembled in Taipei once again. All five hundred thousand servicemen had been reached, and thousands had professed faith in Christ. There were a hundred thousand who completed a Bible study course that required a year of study and memorization. My response to all that God had done was similar to that of David in Psalm 26:7, "That I may publish with the voice of thanksgiving, and tell of all thy wondrous works."

On April 2, 1954, the following letter was written by Madame Chiang Kai-shek.

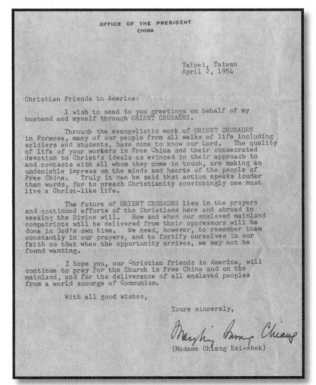

Christian Friends in America:

I wish to send to you greetings on behalf of my husband and myself through ORIENT CRUSADES.

Through the evangelistic work of ORIENT CRUSADES in Formosa, many of our people from all walks of life including soldiers and students, have come to know our Lord. The quality of life of your workers in Free China and their consecrated devotion to Christ's ideals as evinced in their approach to and contacts with all whom they come in touch, are making an undeniable impress on the minds and hearts of the people of Free China. Truly it can be said that action speaks louder than words, for to preach Christianity convincingly one must live a Christ-like life.

The future of ORIENT CRUSADES lies in the prayers and continued efforts of the Christians here and abroad in seeking the Divine will. How and when our enslaved mainland compatriots will be delivered from their oppressors will be done in God's own time. We need, however, to remember them constantly in our prayers, and to fortify ourselves in our faith so that when the opportunity arrives, we may not be found wanting.

I hope you, our Christian friends in America, will continue to pray for the Church in Free China and on the mainland, and for the deliverance of all enslaved peoples from a world scourge of Communism.

With all good wishes,

Yours sincerely,

(Madame Chiang Kai-shek)

TWO WARRIORS MEET

Before our ministry to the army came to an end, I received a cablegram from Dr. Bob Jones Sr., who informed me of his plan to fly to Taiwan with the sole purpose of conferring an honorary doctor's degree on the Generalissimo.

I and hundreds of other people were at the airport in Taipei to meet Dr. Bob's plane. The Madame had a delegation of ladies there to greet him with flowers. Political and military representatives were also there to meet his every need. The crowd was so great I could not get close to him. He finally saw me at a distance and motioned for me to follow him. I followed the procession to the Liberty House, a special guest facility where Chiang Kai-shek entertained dignitaries.

After finally making my way to Dr. Bob's room, I found a guard standing watch. He knocked on the door to see if Dr. Jones wanted to be disturbed. At last I saw him, perspiring profusely, sitting under a ceiling fan with just enough clothes on to "flag a freight train," to use one of his expressions. He said, "Bob, I can't take much more of this—I have never seen so much fuss in all my life." I laughed. "That's what happens when you're famous—now, what can I do for you?" He asked me to send a cablegram to his wife to let her know he had arrived safely and all was well.

Generalissimo Chiang Kai-shek

The Generalissimo (front row—middle) and Dr. Bob Jones Sr. on his right

The next day Dr. Bob, Dr. Leeland Wong, a well-known Chinese evangelist, and I were driven to the home of Chiang Kai-shek. There were a dozen people there, including the Generalissimo, Dr. Bob, Dr. Wong, the U.S. ambassador, and a twenty-two year old missionary, who stood in awe in the presence of giants. It was

11

an honor to meet the man who at one time had been the leader of one-fourth of earth's population.

The ceremony was brief, and the Generalissimo's response still rings in my ears: "Dr. Jones, I have received many degrees from many colleges around the world, but this one means more than all of the others because it is coming from a school that is training young men to preach the gospel of Jesus Christ."

I spoke to Chiang Kai-shek's pastor, Dr. Wei Peng Chen, and asked him if the Generalissimo was a genuine born-again believer. He responded, "Yes, he is truly saved." How good it was to hear that the man who at one time had been the leader of China was a true Christian. Little wonder he had a burden to present the gospel to his army, and little wonder another warrior desired to honor his brother-in-Christ.

CHAPTER THREE
WE CALLED HIM "BILL"

Bill Lee

Following our ministry in the army camps, Dick Hillis suggested we get a taste of island evangelism. About halfway between Taiwan and Mainland China lay a chain of islands called the Pescadores. Twenty-four of them were inhabited. Several of us flew to the main city of Ma-kung with a special young interpreter by our side. He was a good-looking Taiwanese whose father was a pastor in

Kaohsiung, Formosa. His name was Lee Hsin Chang—we called him "Bill." We took turns presenting the gospel to various groups of curious people that assembled. We were quite shocked when one islander asked a member of the team, "This Jesus you are talking about, did He come last year?" Our response was, "No, He came nearly two thousand years ago, and we are sorry you are just now hearing about it."

Most of the team left for Taiwan, but Dick Hillis challenged me to stay on to visit a dozen islands that had never been reached by any missionary. Those islands had never heard the gospel. I found out later that eight of them had never been visited by a white man.

It was necessary to secure a seaworthy vessel, for the task before us required hundreds of miles of travel across ocean that often became turbulent. We found the vessel we needed with its captain and a couple of deck hands. I was the only American onboard, but by my side was a Chinese pastor and some Chinese brothers-in-Christ who had joined us to provide music and share their personal testimonies. Most of all there was my trusted friend and interpreter, "Bill" Lee.

"GOD HAS A MESSAGE FOR US?"

Sitting on top of the cabin of our boat with my arms and legs wrapped around the flagpole, I could view action in the ocean that intrigued the little boy in me. Mighty sharks surfaced and then dived out of sight. There were small, uninhabited islands with thousands of birds nesting in the rocks. Now and then we explored those beautiful creations of God.

It wasn't long until Bill came out of the cabin and said to me as I hung on to my favorite flagpole, "Look ahead—there is our first island. The people there have never heard the name of Jesus." My heart began to pound as we got closer. I could see the people stirring, for they knew visitors were coming.

We dropped anchor past the coral reef. The inquisitive islanders paddled out to our boat and offered to take us to their sandy little island. The news spread quickly that a white man was onboard— they had never seen one before—and it wasn't long until all of the people had gathered. I felt as if I had just landed from Mars. They pinched my white skin and stared into my blue eyes.

The leader of the island asked me, through Bill, "Who are you?" I responded, "I am an American." He said, "But why have you come here?" I replied, "I came because God told me to come." By now he was wide-eyed as he asked, "Why did God tell you to come here?" With joy in my heart I responded, "He asked me to come because He has a message that He wants you and your people to hear." "When can we hear it?" he asked. I answered, "Now." He then said, "Where should we go to hear this message?" Bill and I noticed a Buddhist temple on the highest elevation of the island and suggested we go there for the meeting.

Bill and Bob in front of a Buddhist temple

The leader turned to his people and said, "This man has been sent by God to give us a message. Let's all go to the temple to hear it." The temple site was a perfect location for the meeting since its stairs could serve as a platform and the grassy area was an ideal place for the people to sit. A few minutes later, in front of a Buddhist temple, with pagan idols positioned behind us and curious people seated before us, I told them a story they had never heard—the gospel of the Lord Jesus Christ.

THE FIRST WHITE MAN? NOT REALLY!

The islanders told me that I was the first white man they had ever seen, but then they shocked me when they added, "But you really aren't the first American to come here."

What they meant was that during the days of World War II they had observed American planes as they clashed with the Japanese in deadly dog fights that took place over the very waters where they fished. Many of the planes, American and Japanese, crashed into the salty waters of the Straits of Formosa. After returning home from a successful day of fishing, they would display their catch, which often included great sharks, on the sandy beaches. When those mighty giants of the sea were cut open, they often revealed the skulls and bones of American airmen.

I thanked God for American young men who were willing to respond to the call of Uncle Sam. They even gave their lives for a just cause. But I also wondered where were the young men who were willing to bend their wills to the call of God. How was it that pagan unbelievers could recall the dedication of American soldiers who were willing to die for the cause of freedom, but they were still in spiritual darkness because no one had been willing to go for the cause of Christ?

From one of those islands I wrote to Nan, "There are 300 people on this island, and they have never heard the Gospel of the Lord Jesus. It seems tragic that there should be people like that in the world, but there they were."

A STORM AT SEA

As we journeyed to the next island, I found myself again perched on the roof of the cabin. Suddenly the waves began to swell, and I was hanging on to the flagpole for dear life. Though our little vessel was seaworthy, it was no match for such turbulence. The captain sent Bill to tell me we were being overtaken by a fierce storm and I should come inside. I had already reached that decision. Thoughts were beginning to flood my mind—"Will I ever see my beloved Nan again? What about our marriage and plans for the future?"

A short time later the captain said to Bill, "You had better tell your American friend to hang on—this storm is as bad as I have ever encountered." Things went from bad to worse. Our boat seemed to go straight up then straight down. The captain said, "I fear we will not make it—it looks as if we will sink." "Sink?" I thought. "How can it be? I didn't come to the Orient to sink to the bottom of the ocean. I came to preach God's Word to hungry-hearted people."

Back in Pontiac, Michigan, Mrs. Fred Hunt suddenly awakened. She could not get back to sleep, so she slipped out of bed, fell to her knees, and began to pray. She prayed for Dr. Savage and the needs of the church. She continued to pray for her family, and finally she began praying for missionaries. When she came to my name, she prayed with extra fervency. After an extended period of time she felt peace from the Lord and was confident that all was well. She slipped back into bed and slept through the remainder of the night.

The next Lord's Day she stopped Dad in the hallway of the church. "Rex, will you please write to Bob and ask him why God woke me up in the middle of the night to pray for him?"

Sometime later I received a letter from Dad and discovered that at the same time a Chinese sea captain told us we were about to sink, Mrs. Hunt was on her knees praying. She could not go to a foreign field as a missionary, but she was able to go through prayer. The poet Sandra Goodwin expressed it in these words.

TRAVELING ON MY KNEES

Last night I took a journey
To a land across the seas;
I did not go by boat or plane,
I traveled on my knees.

I saw so many people there
In deepest depths of sin,
But Jesus told me I should go,
That there were souls to win.

But I said, "Jesus, I cannot go
And work with such as these."
He answered quickly, "Yes, you can
By traveling on your knees."

He said, "You pray; I'll meet the need,
You call and I will hear;
Be concerned about lost souls,
Of those both far and near."

And so I tried it, knelt in prayer,
Gave up some hours of ease;
I felt the Lord right by my side
While traveling on my knees.

As I prayed on and saw souls saved
And twisted bodies healed,
And saw God's workers' strength renewed
While laboring on the field.

I said, "Yes, Lord, I have a job,
My desire Thy will to please;
I can go and heed Thy call
By traveling on my knees."

GOD IS ENOUGH

Weeks later and pounds lighter we completed our evangelism on all twelve islands. We returned to the city of Ma-kung on the largest island of the Pescadores. From there the pastor and his people returned to their church. Bill Lee boarded a vessel for Kaohsiung, his hometown in southern Taiwan, and I waited for a DC-3 and my flight back to Taipei. I had a long wait so I rented a room at a nearby Chinese hostel. First, I wrote my daily letter to Nan to tell her how much I loved and missed her. Then I wrote to the Damers to thank them for their sacrificial support and to report all that God had done. I included in the letter a passage from Philippians 4, "Now ye Philippians know also, that in the beginning of the gospel, when I departed from Macedonia, no church communicated with me as concerning giving and receiving, but ye only. For even in Thessalonica ye sent once and again unto my necessity. Not because I desire a gift: but I desire fruit that may abound to your account." I wanted Roger and Louise to know that the great victories that were being wrought would surely abound to their account.

I thought the plane would never come. A cloud of loneliness hung over me. I prayed something like this, "Dear Lord, Bill is gone, so I don't have an interpreter. I can't speak the language of these people and they can't speak English. I really don't have anyone to talk to but You." I discovered something that day that has stayed with me for life—when you have no one but Him, He is enough.

"LEAVE THE RESULTS WITH HIM"

Dick Hillis met me at the airport and drove me back to the mission compound. He didn't share his thoughts with me then, but later he told me I was the most pitiful looking missionary he had ever seen. I had lost several pounds, my clothes needed washing and pressing, and I was physically exhausted. Sometime later I wrote to Nan:

> Dick Hillis was kidding me the other day about you and me
> living in a grass hut out on one of those islands. We might be
> doing just that, Honey. I told him I didn't care where I lived

as long as you were there. Dick said that he learned to love Margaret more than ever when they really roughed it for the Lord. He said that rats had four-lane highways in the walls of their home in China, but those hardships have meant more to them than anything. It may never be that the Lord would call us to live as poorly as Dick and Margaret, Honey, but we must be willing to live any way He wants. We will both be happy under any circumstances knowing that we are in His will. Let's not make drudgery out of it, but let's really put our youth and vitality into the Lord's work.

My time in the Pescadores had been a great experience, but I was a bit perplexed. We had seen thousands come to Christ in the Nationalist Chinese army camps, but I could count on my two hands the number of people who trusted Christ as Savior on the islands. Dick knew I was discouraged. He wisely asked, "Bob, what is the Great Commission?" I responded, "Go into all the world and preach the gospel to every creature." He asked, "Did you do that on the Pescadores?" I replied, "Yes, as best I could." He then said, "Then let's wait and see what God will do . . . let's leave the results with Him."

The apostle Paul once wrote, "I have planted, Apollos watered; but God gave the increase" (I Corinthians 3:6). I was not Paul, but I had planted God's Word on thirsty soil. The Chinese pastor who labored with us was not Apollos, but he went back to those islands and watered the seed that had been planted. It wasn't long until twenty churches sprang up on those twelve islands. Dick Hillis later reported that on one of those little islands with only a hundred families on it over forty families turned to the Lord and burned all of their idols. This proves to me that it isn't the weak ability of the preacher but the powerful Word of God that brings the harvest.

Many years later, I returned to Taiwan at the invitation of American missionaries. When the churches on the Pescadores heard I was back in the area, they invited me to return. Ten delegates came from each of the twenty churches, so we had a conference with two hundred people whom I had preached to in 1952 and who had later come to Christ through the faithful ministry of a national pastor.

The Lord honored His promise in Isaiah 55:11, "So shall my word be that goeth forth out of my mouth: it shall not return unto me void, but it shall accomplish that which I please, and it shall prosper in the thing whereto I sent it."

CHAPTER FOUR
HOME AT LAST

My heart was now burning for the Far East. I knew that as soon as Nan and I were married we would return to this special part of God's harvest field.

Dick Hillis had sent other team members to the Philippines and had decided that that needy land would be the next challenge for the Crusade. He also had a burden for Okinawa and asked if I would pray about returning with Nan to labor in that part of the vineyard. I flew to Okinawa to evaluate the challenge and returned to Taipei with a resounding "Yes, we will go to Okinawa." Now that there were three fields of service, the name of our mission was changed from The Formosa Gospel Crusade to Orient Crusades.

As I stepped off the plane and entered the terminal, I kept search-ing for familiar faces, and then I saw Mom and Dad waving their arms and calling my name. Nan was by their side looking as sweet as ever.

On January 3, 1953, Nan and I were joined as husband and wife in her home church in South Bend, Indiana. My heart pounded as I saw my beautiful bride in her lace and satin coming down the aisle. The wedding party included Cecil Lewis, my friend from college days, who had burst into my room that night and said, "I just saw the girl you are going to marry." I looked at him as the ceremony progressed. He didn't say a word, but from the twinkle in his eye I knew he was saying, "I told you so."

As we stood before the altar arm in arm with heads bowed, we listened as my sister sang a song of consecration by John E. Bode we had chosen for our ceremony.

> O Jesus, [we] have promised to serve Thee to the end;
> Be Thou forever near [us], [Our] Master and [our] Friend:
> [We] shall not fear the battle if Thou art by [our] side,
> Nor wander from the pathway if Thou wilt be [our] guide.
>
> O Jesus, Thou hast promised to all who follow Thee,
> That where Thou art in glory, there shall Thy servant be
> And Jesus, [we] have promised to serve Thee to the end;
> O give [us] grace to follow, [Our] Master and [our] Friend.

MISSIONARY SUPPORT

Following our honeymoon we made our way to the Damer farm. They had attended our wedding and had become like members of our family, but I no longer needed their financial support. Our home churches had expressed their desire to meet our needs.

The trip to the farm was to thank them once again for their faithful giving during my ministry in Taiwan and the Pescadores. When I told them we would be leaving for Okinawa in a few days, Roger said, "Praise the Lord—now we can continue to support you." I probed a bit and discovered that Roger had promised the Lord that as long as I was on the field he would support me. I didn't have the heart to tell him my support was already pledged, so I said to him, "Are you saying you want to continue to support me as a missionary as long as I am on the field?" With a tear in his eye he said, "Yes, I will support you in the future just as I have in the past." Our churches pledged support for Nan, but for ten years every penny of my personal support came from a special farmer and his wife in northern Indiana.

In a letter to the Damers I expressed our heartfelt appreciation,

> Nancy and I were certainly touched as we drove away from your home a few days ago. I am not ashamed to say that we shed a lot of tears before we reached South Bend. They were not tears of sorrow, but tears of thanks to God for such wonderful friends who have stood behind us so faithfully. We love you and thank God for the ministry He has given you. We feel in our hearts that eternity alone will show the tremendous work that God has done through your lives.

OKINAWA

The Hillises and several other couples were in the Far East when our mission changed names, but Nan and I were the first missionaries to leave America to serve under Orient Crusades. We were assigned to evangelize the Ryukyu Islands, a chain of islands that stretch from Japan to Taiwan. There were sixty-three inhabited islands in that chain. We were to make our home on Okinawa, the largest island in the chain.

We landed in the capital city of Naha and were taken to our home—our first home. It was a stucco house that had been built to withstand the fierce typhoons of the Far East. A single missionary named Bob Boardman was living there and continued to do so until his fiancé arrived some months later. They were married and settled into a Japanese-style home nearby.

The first weeks of marriage were a challenge for Nan since she had to cook for three hungry men—Bob Boardman, Bill Lee, and me.

The mission had sent Bill to Okinawa because he was fluent in Japanese and he wanted to continue as my interpreter. Bill's native language was Taiwanese, but he was also proficient in Mandarin, Cantonese, Japanese, and English. At the breakfast table one morning Bill appeared to be tired and puzzled. Nan asked, "Is anything wrong, Bill?" He answered, "Yes, I can't figure out which language to dream in."

Okinawan Christians

School children on Okinawa

Okinawan schools were open to the preaching of the gospel.

Our ministry took us to churches where we preached to open-hearted Christians and to schools where there were receptive young people who were hungry for the gospel. In a letter to the Damers I wrote,

> There are nearly one-hundred and twenty senior and junior
> high schools on Okinawa. We are glad to report that we have
> reached all but one of the twenty-two senior highs and well

over half of the junior highs. I wish you could go with us to some of these high school meetings. We have seen as many as two thousand students, dressed in their black and white uniforms, sit under the hot semitropical sun for an hour without "batting an eyelash." They are hungry for God's Word! These people have been waiting for generations for the life-giving message of salvation in Jesus Christ.

The school meetings take much of our day, but in addition we try to systematically cover the factories, offices, hospitals etc. Almost every evening we are in some village for a special evangelistic service. There have been as many as six or seven hundred of these eager country folks who try to squeeze into a little grass-roofed building. What a joy to preach Christ to such people. The rest of our time is spent among the thirty thousand U.S. servicemen. It would be difficult to give you a mental picture of the American forces on Okinawa.

(November 10, 1953)

Those were the days of the Korean conflict, and Okinawa was the Americans' key base for air operations. Two-thirds of all B-29 bombings in Korea stemmed from Kadena Air Base on Okinawa. When I first visited the island in 1952, I was asked to pray about the possibility of directing a weekly Saturday night rally for U.S. servicemen, called the G.I. Gospel Hour.

Bob Boardman worked with us to handle the follow-up—both to the nationals and to U.S. servicemen. He was an ideal missionary for the task since he had been on Okinawa during World War II as a tank driver in the first marine division. Bob had been seriously wounded and as a result was able to speak with only one vocal chord and the muscles in his throat. What a testimony he was to the Japanese. He was God's servant who whispered the gospel to those who had tried to kill him.

TIME FOR AMERICAN SERVICEMEN

U.S. Air Force chapel, home of the G.I. Gospel Hour

The U.S. Air Force permitted us to use one of their chapels for our Saturday night rally. It wasn't long before men and women from all branches of the service filled the Quonset hut. Their hearts were open and tender. After all, they knew that it was possible that some of them in the chapel on Saturday might be in heaven a few days later.

One airman, a pilot of a B-29 bomber, came to me just prior to a service and said, "Bob, pray for me. I know Christ as Savior but I am not living for Him." He told me he believed the Lord had given him a warning and he wanted to heed it. He said that he was with his crew in a B-29 waiting to take off for Korea to drop their bombs when the base commander radioed and said, "Captain, I do not want you to fly today. I am sending another pilot to take your place." He could not argue with his commander, so he left his crew and plane and another pilot took the controls. His heart sank as he watched his plane take off. He asked the commander why he had refused to let him fly. The commander said simply, "I don't know; I just felt it was the thing to do." Later that day the pilot learned that his plane had been shot down in Korea and no one had survived. Sensing his deep need, I prayed with him, then urged him to move on into a new and intimate walk with Christ. A few days later he flew another bomber with a new crew and never returned.

The work among our U.S. servicemen began to blossom so that before long about 20 percent of our time was spent with Americans. This ministry included the Saturday night rally, Bible study classes, opportunities to take servicemen with us in our ministry to the islands, and a weekly radio broadcast on the armed forces radio service. Nan jokingly told of her husband having a coast-to-coast radio broadcast. Of course, in the middle of Okinawa it was only ten miles from one coast to the other.

Yaka Beach Conference

The men also responded to the opportunity to get off base to attend a conference once or twice a year at Yaka Beach. The U.S. military allowed us to use this R & R facility for our Bible conferences. In a letter to the Damers I wrote,

> I wish you could just get a glimpse of one of the many prostitution areas where our boys are literally spending thousands of dollars each night in such damnable folly. It would break your heart. But amid this sad situation, there are around two hundred and thirty servicemen and women attending a rally every Saturday night that we are directing. Last week, Dick Hillis, director of our mission, and Doug Sparks came up from Formosa to be the special speakers at a three-day Bible Conference for the soldiers, airmen, sailors and WACS. There were one hundred and twenty who attended during the day meetings and around two hundred for each of the evening services. Nearly fifty decisions were made for salvation, full-time service and re-dedication. Never have I seen such spiritual hunger among American people.

Though more than fifty years have slipped by since those days on Okinawa, we still see the results of the power of God's Word in the lives of our servicemen. Some of them returned to the States, entered Christian colleges, and are currently serving the Lord as pastors and missionaries.

CHAPTER FIVE
BON VOYAGE

About midway through our term on Okinawa the Lord blessed us with our first child—a precious little girl we named Rebecca. She became the darling of our Okinawan friends as well as our Gospel Hour servicemen.

Bob and Jean Boardman (left) with Bob, Nan, and Becky

Becky was a delight to "Uncle Bill," and before long a special bond developed between the two of them. Years later the Lord led Hsue Hsu, a beautiful Taiwanese girl into Bill's life. He gave her an American name—"Becky." Lee Shin Chang and Hsue Hsu are two of our dearest friends today. Of course, we still call them Bill and Becky.

Bill and Becky

Bill and I began spending more and more time on the islands. It was a delight to watch the people assemble. Some men came straight from their rice fields, others from fishing boats. Ladies often arrived with babies on their backs. The mothers agilely bounced along with their little ones snugly wrapped in their brightly colored pouches. The hearts of the people were open, and everywhere we went crowds gathered to hear the gospel story. Many professed faith in Christ. Bob Boardman had set up an office with several national workers to handle the follow-up ministry. It wasn't long before there were ten thousand Okinawans studying God's Word through the Bible correspondence course.

Bon voyage

The work on Okinawa and throughout the Ryukyus was developing into a greater challenge than we had ever envisioned. The only "down side" for me was the necessity of leaving Nan and Becky for extended periods of time. Whenever the time came for another trip to the islands, Nan, Becky, and I would bounce down the rough road in our carry-all to the docks. Bill, and occasionally one of our servicemen, would be there ready to board a small Japanese ship for our journey. With sad music playing on the PA system, the ship would slowly move away from the pier. I, like everyone else on the ship, held a roll of brightly colored crepe paper in my hand with Nan holding on to the other end. As the ship pulled away, the streamers would begin to unroll until finally they would break. It was then we were officially on our way.

Nan, with Becky in her arms, bravely returned to our carry-all and began her short journey back to our home.

> Waves of loneliness began to sweep over me as we left the dock. Once again there would be the adjustments of having my faithful companion many miles away. Caring for little Becky kept me occupied and amused most of the time, but still there was that longing for times of sweet communion with my loved one.
>
> During the days of separation, I would often be reminded of the commitment I made to the Lord at the age of 19. I had come to the crossroads in my life when I had to choose between two masters—which one would I serve. It was during an evangelistic service that I surrendered my life and will to Christ, promising Him to always do His will no matter what it involved or where it would take me.
>
> Now, it was clear, this was His will for me at this time—to be a faithful wife, mother, and encourager to my mate in fulfilling his God-given calling.

AN UNWANTED VISITOR

The challenge of reaching the people on the Ryukyus with the gospel was an extraordinary opportunity. Added to the loneliness of being away from Nan and Becky for long periods was the concern that I felt following an experience that Nan had with an unwanted visitor.

That evening was no different from any other. After Becky was bathed and tucked into bed, I proceeded to prepare for my night's sleep. Since the mosquitoes on Okinawa carried a dreaded disease called encephalitis, it was necessary that we drape mosquito nets over our beds. After a time of prayer I turned out the light, crawled under the net, and went sound asleep.

Because of the dampness in the closets it was necessary to keep a light bulb, covered with a metal net, burning at all times. The closet door kept the light from shining into our room. In the middle of the night, I sensed that a light was on somewhere, but I didn't check it out and went back to sleep. I didn't know that at that very moment a thief was in my bedroom closet stealing mission money from a briefcase. He must have heard the bed creak and left hurriedly.

When I awakened the next morning, I went to the kitchen to prepare for breakfast and was shocked to see the window screens resting on the floor. Then I noticed broken glass on the cement floor in the dining room. After piecing everything together, the terrifying thought finally dawned on me—someone had broken into the house. Rushing to Becky's bedroom to see if she was all right, I found her window wide open where the thief had escaped. Then I checked my bedroom and opened the closet to find papers scattered and the money gone. I was so stunned that I hardly knew what to do next. Immediately I shared what had happened with our missionary neighbors, and they were a great comfort to me. How I longed for my loving husband to be there to hold me, but I knew that he wouldn't be home for another week from the islands. There was no way to communicate with him, but there was one Friend I could call on—the one Who said, "I will never leave thee nor forsake thee."

Even though I now had great peace from the Lord, I felt I should take certain precautions such as moving Becky's bed into my room and locking the bedroom door upon retiring. How wonderful it was to sense God's omnipotent hand of protection through an experience that He no doubt had allowed for my good.

Having heard of my experience, a GI from the Gospel Hour offered to give us his pet cocker spaniel to be our watchdog. Since the young man was leaving for the States, he was happy to find a good home for Windy. It wasn't long before this new member of the family proved to be just what we needed.

Nan, Becky, and Windy

In one of Nan's letters home she wrote, "The other night at 3:00 we woke up when we heard someone rattling the front windows. Bob sneaked into the living room in the dark and watched the intruder trying to get the window open. The thing that he didn't know is that my hubby put locks on each window. I think Bob was proud to think that his idea worked." Nan forgot to mention to my parents that I unleashed Windy, who then pursued the intruder. The thief was so scared that he ran over the embankment in our backyard, screaming at the top of his lungs with Windy nipping at his heels.

NAN WAS LOOKING

It was a blessing beyond description to preach God's Word in tiny villages and schools on distant islands, but I was always eager to return to Nan and Becky. I was careful to give Nan the time of our return, but we soon learned that the ships rarely arrived on schedule.

> As the time for Bob's return approached I began to share my excitement with Becky. "Daddy is coming home," I would say. It was a thrill to see the twinkle in her eyes. When the day arrived, I began looking every few minutes for his ship. Our home was perched on top of a hill that overlooked the city of Naha and the harbor. When at last I would see in the distance a ship that appeared to be the right one, I would put a frilly little dress on Becky, place her in the car seat of our carry-all, and drive down the rough road to the dock just in time to meet the wrong ship. Sometimes we would meet several ships before the one we longed for finally arrived.

One of our servicemen heard of Nan's frequent trips to the docks, so he got my attention after a Saturday night meeting and asked, "Have you ever heard of binoculars?" I answered, "Yes, of course!" He then handed me a pair and said, "It's my gift to Nan—from now on she will be able to identify your ship."

Nan waiting

Some weeks later as I was returning home after a fruitful ministry on a distant island, Okinawa suddenly came into view. Then my eyes focused on the quaint little city of Naha. It wasn't long before I could see a tiny dot on top of a hill—it was my home. I couldn't see Nan, but I knew she was looking. My bride was anxious for my return, and it thrilled my heart. I could imagine how our Lord will respond when He comes for His waiting bride.

"I DON'T NEED YOU ANYMORE"

About a year-and-a-half after the Lord gave us Becky, He brought another precious bundle into our lives. We named her Sharon Kay. Her curly auburn hair often caught the eyes of our Okinawan friends and, like Becky, she never lacked for love or attention. Of course, we were eager to present Becky and Shari to their grandparents, but one final challenge was before us before leaving Okinawa.

I had been burdened for some time about Bill Lee's future. He had been my faithful interpreter for years as I labored in Taiwan, the Pescadores, and now the Ryukyus. Bill had expressed his desire to be my interpreter for life.

Dick Hillis had been challenged by the Christian and Missionary Alliance (C&MA), the pioneer mission society in Southeast Asia, to come to Viet Nam. Dick asked me to pray about directing the work of O.C. in this new field. Nan and I felt a strong tug from the Holy Spirit to take the challenge. This meant that after furlough we would be going to Viet Nam without Bill.

A village meeting in northern Okinawa

Bill and I were in an isolated village in northern Okinawa. The service had been well announced, so we expected the entire village to be present that evening. We went to the meeting place to prepare for the outdoor service. The tailgate on the carry-all would be used for a platform. Just before the service as people began to assemble, I asked Bill, "What are you going to do with your life?" He thought for a moment and replied, "I plan to be your interpreter." I then shared our plans to return to the States for furlough and then go to Viet Nam. "Bill, Nan and I are going to learn Vietnamese; furthermore, that is one language you don't know, so your days to serve as my interpreter are nearly over. What do you feel God wants you to do?" After a long silence he said, "I believe He wants me to preach His Word." I said, "I have thought that for quite some time, so why don't you begin tonight." He gasped. "You mean I should preach tonight by myself?" "Yes, Bill," I responded, "I will be out of sight praying for you."

A short while later, Bill stood before the people of that village and proclaimed the gospel story. At the invitation eighteen people came forward to receive Christ as Savior. When the people left and Bill and I were alone, I said, "Bill, that was wonderful. God's hand was on you." To this day I can still hear him say, "Yes, you are right, so I don't need you anymore." "That's right," I answered, "what you need is the power of the Holy Spirit and a knowledge of His Word. Get on with the work, Bill; I know great days are ahead for you."

During our one-year furlough Bill led over five hundred Okinawans to Christ. He later pastored a trilingual church in Tokyo with Japanese, Chinese, and Americans in his congregation. Ten years later he and Hsue Hsu moved to New York City. During the twenty years that followed, Bill started four churches among Taiwanese immigrants.

FURLOUGH

Our return to the States was one of the most memorable events of our lives. When we stepped off the plane in Detroit, Michigan, with two daughters our parents had never seen, it was like all heaven broke loose. To this day Nan says that that experience was one of the greatest of her life.

Furlough was a busy time with many meetings and much travel. The little boy who said, "When I grow up, I want to be a missionary home on furlough," certainly knew nothing of its demands. It was during furlough that the news came of the deaths of five young men on the banks of the Curaray River in Ecuador. One of them was Ed McCully, who had married Marilou Hobolth, a young lady in our youth group at First Baptist in Pontiac. Another member of that team of five young missionaries was Jim Elliot.

Years earlier when I was traveling with the BJU quartet we were scheduled for a service in Illinois. It was my privilege not only to sing in the quartet but also to preach. Little did I realize that two of the young men in that service, Jim Elliot and Ed McCully, would later be martyred for Christ's sake in Ecuador.

One of my final services on furlough was a youth rally in the state of Washington. I was there to challenge the young people regarding the task of world evangelism. Jim Elliot's father was there to give his personal testimony and the account of his son's martyrdom at the hands of Auca Indians. Following the service, Mr. Elliot came to me and said, "I can't pray for Jim anymore, but I can and will pray for you." What an honor it was to receive such a promise from such a man of God.

The year had flown by and the day arrived for our return to the Orient. As our family gathered at the depot in Pontiac, Nan, the girls and I boarded the train for California with heavy hearts. We were thrilled to be going to Viet Nam but saddened to think that we would not see our loved ones for four years. It was especially difficult for Mom and Dad since Becky and Shari were their only grandchildren.

As we pressed our noses against the windows of our coach, it began to snow. The flakes were big and those standing on the platform were soon covered. The train slowly pulled away from the station. My dad wasn't waving good-by; he appeared instead to be pushing us forward. It was not a motion to stay but to go. He was saying, "My heart aches to see you leave, but I know it is God's will. It's time for you to go."

Years later from Viet Nam I wrote these words to Mom and Dad, "We praise the Lord for you—more than ever. The Lord is someday going to reward you for the terrific spirit you have taken in being separated from your children. We love you for it."

I have the conviction that in every missionary conference there should be a time to honor the parents and grandparents of mission-aries. After all, it is one thing to go—it is another thing to let go.

CHAPTER SIX
ARRIVAL IN VIET NAM

After a train ride to California, a flight to the Philippines, and an adventure on a French ship to Viet Nam, we finally arrived in Saigon. In a newsletter dated March 1957, I wrote,

> Our hearts skipped a beat as we got the first glimpse of the beautiful land of Viet Nam, our home and place of ministry. The voyage from Manila to Saigon was interesting, but the sight of flying fish and blue water could not compare to the beautiful mountains along the coast of Viet Nam. It took our French ship several hours of inland sailing on the Saigon River before we reached the city of Saigon. "The Paris of the Orient" is the name often used to describe Saigon. This is no doubt due to the fact that Saigon (now the capital) was a very important city of French Indo-China during the years of French rule.

The C&MA missionaries were there to greet us as we walked off the ship. They took us to the receiving home and treated us royally. Becky and Shari were excited to be with other "MKs." It was as if they had been bosom buddies from birth.

Becky, Shari, and Dan on our compound in Saigon

Nan and I rejoice to this day for the way our children responded to life on the mission field. Becky and Shari adjusted quickly and had no ill effects. Later, to our delight, the Lord gave us a son, whom we named Dan. He, like his sisters, felt very much at home in the land of his birth. Years before we went to Viet Nam, while I was still an unmarried, lovesick missionary in Taiwan, I wrote to Nan, "I'm beginning to think that the mission field is as good as any place to raise a family." What I thought to be true then I discovered to be true later.

When the children of Israel complained that their children would suffer as the result of their move from Egypt to Canaan, God declared, "Your little ones, which ye said should be a prey, them will I bring in" (Numbers 14:31). I wrote in the margin of my Bible, "God can take care of our children." Indeed He did!

Our mission had purchased a beautiful compound with two duplexes. Three of the units were for family housing, and the fourth unit served as our office for the follow-up ministry. Missionary Warren Myers was already settled, and the office was staffed with Vietnamese workers who could handle the correspondence school.

Quang and his wife-to-be

The Lord brought into my life a young man who would be to my ministry in Viet Nam what Bill Lee had been earlier. Tran Xuan Quang was not only my interpreter but also my language teacher, for it was my goal to be able to preach God's Word to the Vietnamese in their own language. Even through the years of language study I was able to carry on in the work of evangelism because of Brother Quang.

In a letter to the Damers dated November 12, 1959, I was finally able to report, "I preached my first message in Vietnamese last Sunday morning in one of the churches here in Saigon. It is a real thrill to be able to talk to the people in their own tongue. I can't say

ARRIVAL IN VIET NAM

it was absolutely perfect—I guess all the words were pronounced correctly, but there was certainly a lot missing as far as the spirit of the message was concerned. So, just keep praying that Nan and I will enjoy the freedom in the language and be able to get close to the hearts of these people."

VIET NAM AND MISSIONARY PIONEERS

The year was 1893. France had completed her conquest of Cambodia, Viet Nam, and Laos and had given birth to a new colony called French Indo-China. Cambodia was the first to fall, then Viet Nam capitulated in 1883, and finally Laos came under French rule in 1893. That was also the year that A. B. Simpson, founder of a mission society called the Christian and Missionary Alliance (out of which grew the denomination) made his trip around the world. His burden for French Indo-China was evident in his report, which said in part, "The southeastern peninsula of Asia has been much neglected. The great kingdom of An Nam should be occupied for Christ."

Dr. R. A. Jaffray was the first missionary to respond to Simpson's plea. He arrived in Viet Nam in 1911. There were other pioneers who followed Jaffray, and though they were up in years when we arrived in 1957, they were still active and effective in their ministry.

Some of them had served in the northern part of the country, but when the French were defeated and the nation was divided at the seventeenth parallel in 1954, they, like one million Vietnamese living in the north, moved to the south.

When the political dust had settled, there was a Communist nation called North Viet Nam under the rule of Ho Chi Minh and a freedom-loving nation called South Viet Nam under the leadership of Ngo Dinh Diem.

THEY ROWED THEIR BOATS

Christians in Viet Nam were doctrinally sound, fervent in spirit, and active in their local churches. I wrote of one of the churches in a newsletter dated January 1958.

> Dear Friends,
>
> Pastor Hen of the church at Sadec, Viet Nam, visited me a few weeks ago. During the course of our conversation I learned that his church is situated near the famous Mekong River, one of the longest in the world. This great river begins in Tibet and winds like a serpent through Laos, Cambodia and Viet Nam before emptying into the South China Sea.
>
> There are one-hundred Christians in his church, fifty of whom live along this great winding river. These Christians love the fellowship of the church so they leave their homes around two or three o'clock every Sunday morning and row from three to five hours, depending on the current.
>
> The Sunday morning bulletin, if they had one, would read like this:
>
> 7:30—Prayer service
>
> 8:30—Teachers meet for instruction
>
> 9:30—Youth meeting
>
> 10:30—Sunday School
>
> 11:15—Morning worship service

After lunch and a bit of good Christian fellowship, they get in their boats and row from three to five hours arriving back home shortly before dark. Fifty percent of this church faithfully carry on the above routine.

Compare this with the Sunday schedule of the average Christian in America. These dear Christians laboriously row in the dark for five hours before most of us get out of bed on Sunday morning. And then the thought of a church having meetings from 7:30 until noon is enough to make one move his membership or, better still, just catch a 30-minute sermonette by radio and call it quits for the week.

Next Sunday, on your way to church in your car, remember these fifty Christians who will be rowing their little boats for eight hours so that they, like you, may fellowship with other believers in the bonds of our Lord Jesus Christ.

Because of Calvary,

Bob Shelton

A church gathering in Nha Trang, Viet Nam

DOG FOR DINNER

Though Nan, the children, and I lived in Saigon, my ministry took me from the DMZ in the north to the Mekong Delta in the south. Our mission was to assist the national church, called the Hoi Thanh Tin Lanh, in the work of evangelism.

There were a few times when we did some pioneer work where there were no missionaries or national believers. Quang and I found ourselves in such a place on one occasion. Permission had been given to use the public hall, so we advertised the meeting throughout the village with our PA system.

As the afternoon wore on, a hospitable family invited us to have dinner with them. Their home with its thatched roof and dirt floor reflected their poverty as did the meal they offered, but Quang and I appreciated their kindness and proceeded to eat what was put before us.

We thanked them for their kindness and the meal, then excused ourselves so that we could get ready for the service. As we sat in our Land Rover going over the message that I would be preaching and Quang would be interpreting, we suddenly began to feel strange—then sick. I turned to Quang and asked, "What did we eat tonight?" He knew but wouldn't tell me (later I learned it was dog). Finally I said, "Quang, I don't think I can preach." He responded, "That's good because I won't be able to interpret."

We bowed our hearts before the one who had brought us to that village and prayed, "Dear Lord, these people need Your Word, and we believe You have brought us here to give it to them. Give us Your strength and use us for Your glory."

We were so weak we could hardly walk to the platform. Our strength was completely gone, but in our weakness we stood before those hungry-hearted Vietnamese and began to preach. The Holy Spirit provided the physical strength to present the gospel, and His anointing was upon us as we told them the most blessed story they had ever heard. We could say with the apostle Paul: "And he said unto me, My grace is sufficient for thee: for my strength is made perfect in weakness. Most gladly therefore will I rather glory in my infirmities, that the power of Christ may rest upon me" (II Corinthians 12:9).

Quang and I will never cease to praise the Lord for what He accomplished in that service. Fifty-three Vietnamese trusted Christ as Savior and were born into the family of God. They became the "pillars" of a church that remains to this day.

CHAPTER SEVEN
THE CONVICTION WAS STRONG— I MUST GO

Tom Stebbins and his brother George were working together in Tuy Hoa. They had both been brought up in Viet Nam as MKs and had returned under different missions to work with the people they had learned to love. I received a letter from Tom inviting me to come to Tuy Hoa for a tent crusade, so I purchased a train ticket and was scheduled for the three-hundred-mile night trip from Saigon to Tuy Hoa.

The conviction was strong—I must go.

On the afternoon prior to my departure, I was sitting in my office going over materials for the crusade when there was a knock at the door—it was Mrs. Ruth Jeffrey. Mrs. Jeffrey and her husband, Ivory, were two of those pioneer missionaries who had blazed the trail for Christ in Viet Nam. Ruth, like so many missionaries, was also an MK—her father was Jonathan Goforth of China. The Jeffreys had urged Dick Hillis to send missionaries to Viet Nam to assist them in evangelism, so she felt a particular burden for our ministry.

There was much unrest in South Viet Nam in those days because the Viet Cong, Communists living in the south but taking orders from Ho Chi Minh in the north, were very active in their guerilla warfare.

Mrs. Jeffrey said, "Bob, I just heard that you are leaving tonight by train to go to Tuy Hoa. Are you sure this is God's will? Have you heard how the Viet Cong are stopping some of those trains in search of government officials and Americans? I just want you to know I am concerned, but if you go I will be praying for you."

We prayed together and she left. In a matter of minutes our little two-year-old son, Dan, came into my office. He climbed up on my lap and in his limited vocabulary shared with me what he and the other children were doing. We chatted for a minute and the visit was over. Away he went to join his compound buddies and their next earth-shaking adventure.

With Mrs. Jeffrey's concern and the reminder of my responsibilities as a father, I bowed my heart before the Lord and pleaded for His peace to go or stay. The conviction was strong; I must go.

The ride that night to Tuy Hoa was uneventful. I even slept as the train made its way from Saigon northward along the coast of the South China Sea. It arrived in Tuy Hoa at the appointed time. The blessing of God upon the tent crusade will stay with me forever. I returned to Saigon with John 10:4 burning in my heart, "When He putteth forth His own sheep, He goeth before them . . ."

Tent crusade, Tuy Hoa, Viet Nam

Not long after the trip to Tuy Hoa the Communists not only stopped the train but also turned it onto its side in their mad search for government officials and Americans.

THE CONCENTRATION CAMP

The trip to Tuy Hoa resulted not only in a blessed tent crusade but also in an unusual opportunity to present the gospel in a setting I had never thought possible. An officer in the Vietnamese army approached Tom Stebbins and suggested that I preach to a group of Communist captives who were being held at a concentration camp nearby.

My first silent response was "Why should I preach the gospel to such wicked people? After all, they were murdering innocent Vietnamese—some of them Christians." The Viet Cong had paved the way for the North Vietnamese regular troops in Ho Chi Minh's bid to take over South Viet Nam.

By the time the war ended in 1975, fifteen American missionaries had been killed or taken captive, never to be seen again. One of those in Ban Me Thuot was Ruth Thompson, Tom Stebbins's sister. Many others were martyred at the hands of ruthless Communists. Some were pastors with whom I had labored. Many tribal believers were skinned alive and their skins were hung on the trees of central Viet Nam. Other believers were buried alive.

My first response to the request to preach to a group of captured Communists was much like the response of Jonah when God commissioned him to preach to the Ninevites. I complained to the Lord, "They don't deserve to be saved." God reminded me from His Word that I didn't deserve salvation either and that His command to "go into all the world and preach the gospel to every creature" had not changed.

Tom and I got into a Vietnamese jeep and were driven to the concentration camp. Guards opened the barbed wire gate to allow us to enter. Before us was a large pavilion where hundreds of Communists were seated on a concrete floor. I presented the gospel to eager listeners who seemed to grasp the need for God's Son to come to earth so that He might take upon Himself the sin of the whole world. I explained the necessity for them to come to

Christ as penitent sinners and then to accept this crucified and resurrected Son of God as their personal savior.

That day several Communists turned from their sin and professed to receive Christ as Savior. Yes, God can save a Ninevite or a Communist.

LORD OF THE VIETNAMESE JUNGLE

It was often my joy to go into the central highlands to minister to the Montagnards. John and Jo Newman were with our mission and were enjoying a fruitful ministry among those tribal people. A generation before they had been headhunters, but missionaries like Herb and Lydia Jackson and Gordon and Laura Smith had pioneered the tribal ministry and thousands had come to Christ. In some instances entire villages had come to the Lord. We called them Christian villages.

Tribal village

Tribal church

John Newman had arranged for me to conduct a series of meetings in one of the villages. After the meetings were over, the tribal pastor shared his concern for the safety of his people. A large Bengal tiger had been lurking in the jungle near the village rice fields.

Tigers are beautiful creatures and deserve the right to survive, but now and then a tiger will become a man-eater. If not killed, he will kill. About five hundred South Viet Nam tribal people were killed each year by tigers.

The people had become fearful to go out at night or to work their rice fields during the day. Since the South Vietnamese government would not permit tribal people to own guns, the pastor asked John and me to try to kill the tiger. John had his gun along, but he had already killed a man-eater, so he tossed the weapon into my lap and said, "This one is yours!"

When nightfall came, we put on our lights, which were similar to coal miners' headlamps. We began our search, but with only one gun between us I was an uneasy missionary. I must confess that I really didn't want to come face to face with the "lord of the Vietnamese jungle."

We returned to the village and reported our failure in finding the tiger. The pastor said, "That's fine; we have another plan." The next day the men of the village led a sickly horse into the jungle. When they reached a certain place, several miles from the village, they killed the horse and secured it to a young sapling at the base of a large tree. Then they constructed a ladder that reached to the crotch of the tree, where they built a platform.

They returned to the village with the news that the bait was in place and the platform was built. The pastor then said, "In a few days the bait will be ripe." That would be my cue to climb the tree and wait for the hungry tiger. The pastor was right; in a few days the bait was "ripe." My, was it ripe! I went to the site, climbed up the ladder, and sat on my perch about twenty feet over the bait.

Lord of the Vietnamese jungle

Climbing to my platform

That evening was tranquil. The sun was beginning to set. The sound of tropical birds singing their songs was indescribable. I wondered if God had told His jungle creatures to put on a special concert for His servant.

Suddenly the sun disappeared, the birds ended their concert, and jungle sounds, not so pleasant, could be heard. The jungle floor was so dark I could no longer see the bait. Then I heard the sound of a large animal crashing through a growth of dry bamboo. I could hear him breathe and lick the bait, but I couldn't see him. I pointed the gun toward the bait and was about to turn on my head lantern when I remembered John's counsel, "Wait until he starts to eat before you turn on the light and shoot."

I waited and waited but could no longer hear him. He had left without a sound. He came like an elephant and left like a ghost. A few minutes later he returned and again I could hear him breathing and licking the bait just twenty feet below me, but the second time he left without a sound. I climbed down out of the tree, looked at his paw prints in the dirt, and returned to the village. The tiger had made his claim and would surely return, but since I had a commitment in Saigon the next day, I had to leave.

When I arrived at the jungle site the following day, I was saddened to discover that the tiger had returned the night I was gone and had almost completely devoured that full-grown horse. No doubt he later succeeded in killing several of my tribal friends. I could see a parallel with our conflict with Satan. The truth of I Peter 5:8 is still true, "Be sober, be vigilant; because your adversary the devil, as a roaring lion, walketh about, seeking whom he may devour."

LEPER COLONIES

My first encounter with lepers came during a visit to Okinawa before Nan and I were married. In a letter to Mom and Dad I wrote, "I spent last Tuesday in a leper colony on a little peninsula fifty miles north of here. There are 924 lepers there. I preached to the Christians, and could hardly keep back the tears. Those lepers were singing God's praises. Some of them had no fingers, hands had been eaten away, feet were gone, eyes lost and faces disfigured."

This Okinawan Christian leper said to me, "I praise the Lord for this disease, for I would never have come to Christ if I had not become a leper."

A meeting with lepers in a wooded area of their colony

That meeting had been held in a wooded area some distance from the village. As I waited for all of the people to arrive, I noticed one man groping along trying to find his way to the clearing. Just then, a nearby leper became aware of his blind friend's struggle and led him to the meeting place.

As I was leaving the peninsula, I couldn't help but notice wives and children standing at the gate tearfully bidding farewell to their forlorn loved ones in the colony. Leprosy is a cruel disease that brings separation.

Years later, I was invited by Mrs. Lillian Dickson to speak at a leprosarium near Taipei, Taiwan. As soon as I arrived, she shared her excitement over a supply of cots that had recently arrived. Since most Taiwanese sleep on woven mat floors, I asked why the exuberance over the beds for "her lepers." She said, "Oh, don't you know that leprosy eventually leaves a person without feeling?" She went on to explain how rats entered the dorms at night and literally nibbled away fingers and toes without the sleeping lepers feeling a thing. Leprosy renders a person insensitive.

A leper in Viet Nam made this cross for me. He had no fingers.

During our term in Viet Nam I spoke in the mountain tribal city of Ban Me Thuot. The first meeting was held in the little thatch-roofed tribal church where my close friend Bob Ziemer was laboring. (Years later, it was in this city that the Communists invaded the missionary compound and confronted Bob as he tried to plead for the lives of his comrades. They shot and killed Bob and then went on to hurl grenades into the bunker where other missionaries were hiding. In all, six missionaries from that compound were martyred.)

In the jungle a few miles from the tribal church was a leper colony. My friend Archie Mitchell was eager for me to speak to "his lepers" concerning the coming of Christ. (Later Communist troops stormed the area and captured Archie, Dr. Ardel Vietti, and Dan Gerber and then led them into the jungle—never to be seen again.) With the lepers seated before me on log benches, I remember speaking of our Lord's return for His bride, when we shall be caught up to meet Him in the air. I labored the point that before we are caught up we shall be changed—given glorified, perfect, incorruptible bodies. Just then, one disfigured leprous lady took her fingerless hand and nudged her neighbor as if to say, "Did you hear that?"

Leprosy in Scripture is presented as a type of sin; however, this does not mean that a person with leprosy is more of a sinner than anyone else. It simply means that leprosy does to the human body what sin does to the soul. If not treated, it blinds, separates, renders a person insensitive, and results in death.

CHAPTER EIGHT
A GREAT DOOR...MANY ADVERSARIES

Anti-Communist sign

The apostle Paul wrote, "For a great door and effectual is opened unto me, and there are many adversaries" (I Corinthians 16.9). I had never experienced the reality of this verse more than in a special little city in the Mekong Delta called Bac Lieu. Quang and I were there to conduct an eight-day campaign in the Hoi Thanh Tin Lanh church. The first services on Sunday were well attended and the blessing of God came pouring down like rain from heaven.

When God is doing something, Satan does his best to interfere. Prior to the Monday evening service several believers shared with us their stories of horror. We heard of relatives who were shot and neighbors who were murdered. It seemed the Viet Cong were everywhere, doing whatever they wanted to do. The war with North Viet Nam had not begun, but the guerilla warfare of the VC was in full swing.

On Friday afternoon the Viet Cong slipped into the city of Bac Lieu, caught the mayor as he rode his bicycle down main street, slit his throat, and left as quickly as they came. The mayor died on the spot before his horrified people.

That evening we prepared for what we thought might be our final service. We had originally planned and had announced a Sunday through Sunday campaign; but with so much confusion and heartache, we thought it best to conclude on Friday night. As the service was about to begin, down the middle aisle came a group of unidentified men. Since the only seats available were on the front row, that is where they sat. The pastor left the platform and joined the deacons at the back of the church.

We didn't sing as much as usual, and I didn't preach as long as usual because I knew the people were troubled about our uninvited guests. I was also a bit concerned because all the time I was preaching I noticed the pastor and deacons had their eyes glued to that front row of men.

When the service ended, the people left as quickly as they could and the unidentified men also slipped away. The pastor, Quang, and I met at the front of the church. "Who were those men on the front row?" I asked the pastor. He replied, "I think they were VC, perhaps the very men who murdered our mayor this afternoon." "Why did they come to our service?" "They know you are sleeping in the church," he replied, "and we believe they will be back later tonight to kill you."

The South Vietnamese government had notified the chairman of the C&MA that they had intercepted a communiqué from the Communist government in Hanoi to the Viet Cong. In essence, it said that soon the order would be given to start killing American missionaries.

When the pastor told me he expected the VC to return later that evening to kill me, I then asked, "What do you suggest?" He responded, "I don't think you should sleep in the church." "I don't either—where should I sleep?"

The pastor had already made arrangements for me to spend the night with one of the families in the church. A few minutes later the deacons were back with a cyclo, the Vietnamese version of the Chinese rickshaw. As Quang and I climbed into the cyclo, the pastor and all the deacons mounted their bicycles and formed a circle around us. With our bicycle escort, we made our way to the home of the family that had volunteered to have us spend the night.

After a time of reading God's Word and praying with this courageous family, they took me to my room. It was small, but private. I crawled under the mosquito net that hung from the ceiling, turned off the little light at the head of the bed, and tried to sleep, but to no avail. I felt confident the Communists knew where I was and I would not see the light of another day.

Falling to my knees, I began to plead with the Lord for more time to serve Him and to be the husband, father, and missionary I believed He wanted me to be. Finally, in the middle of the night I read from Psalm 91, "Thou shalt not be afraid for the terror by night; nor for the arrow that flieth by day . . . There shall no evil befall thee, neither shall any plague come nigh thy dwelling. For He shall give His angels charge over thee, to keep thee in all thy ways." I was more aware than ever before that my times are in God's hand.

A special peace from the Lord swept over my soul, and I knew He was in control. The next morning Quang and I walked to the church and continued the campaign through Sunday evening. I learned in Bac Lieu that the place of God's choosing is the safest place on earth.

A GIFT FROM INDIA

It was a beautiful day in Saigon. As I was in my office studying, one of our national workers came charging in with an announcement that would change the course of my day. "A plane is about to land at the airport with a special gift from the Buddhists of India to the Buddhists of Viet Nam," he exclaimed. When he told me what the gift was, I responded, "Let's go!"

Our mission compound was a few minutes from Saigon's Tan Son Nhut airport. Hundreds of faithful Buddhists were there awaiting the arrival of the plane. It wasn't long until someone shouted,

"There it is." The plane descended and finally landed. It slowly taxied toward the crowd and came to a stop at a special designated parking place. A red carpet was laid, the door opened, and out walked a group of brightly robed monks carrying the coveted gift. It was in a beautifully colored urn, so we could not see the gift, but we knew what it was—a bone of Buddha.

Tom Stebbins later told me he saw this special gift covered with gold in a glass case in a temple in Da Nang. Buddha's remains have found their way to sacred temples around the world. According to Bill Lee, one of Buddha's teeth had been flown to Taiwan. A crowd of a hundred thousand people gathered and bowed before that tiny object.

The question is often asked, "Are these human remains actually parts of Buddha's body?" Tom Stebbins was quick to say that all he saw was gold encasing what was believed to be a bone of Buddha. Whether the people of Viet Nam saw his real bone is not the vital issue. Buddhists believe their leader had no victory over death.

As my Vietnamese coworker and I observed faithful Buddhists bowing before a bone, I turned to him and whispered, "How good to know we can't fly a bone of Jesus into Viet Nam today. Our Savior arose from the dead."

The songwriter expressed it in these words,

> Living, He loved me; dying, He saved me;
> Buried, He carried my sins far away;
> Rising, He justified freely forever:
> One day He's coming—O glorious day!

"LET'S NOT BE ROMANTIC"

In addition to conducting meetings in local churches and crusades that sometimes required tents and auditoriums, we would occasionally invite missionaries from other countries to come to Viet Nam for special campaigns. On one occasion we invited missionary David Morken and a team of musicians—Gene and Dean Denler from Hong Kong and Norm Nelson from the Philippines—to come to Saigon for an area-wide crusade.

About half-way through the meetings, David asked if I thought it possible to meet President Ngo Dinh Diem. I told him that probably the president was too busy to see us, but I would write a letter to make the request.

I was shocked when South Viet Nam's president answered my letter with a warm response. He said he would be happy to see us. At the appointed time, David and I arrived at the beautiful white palace in Saigon for our meeting with President Diem.

The palace guard escorted us down a hallway to a room where the president met his guests. It wasn't long before the door opened and in walked the president of South Viet Nam. He invited us to be seated and immediately began to speak of his concern about the impending war with North Viet Nam. He spoke of the Communist troops that were beginning to infiltrate the central highlands. Then he went on to explain the movements of other North Vietnamese soldiers that were taking the water route and entering South Viet Nam at the Mekong Delta. We could see the concern on his face and sensed the anxiety in his heart as he told us it would not be long until the war with Ho Chi Minh's forces would begin.

President Ngo Dinh Diem with Dave Morken and Bob

After a time I said to the president that I believed God had directed us to him that day to assure him of our prayer support and also to tell him of God's love. I proceeded to share with him the gospel story with its message of Bethlehem, Calvary, and the tomb. I explained that if he would open his heart to the crucified and resurrected Son of God, he would not only have life everlasting but also wisdom from above to conduct the fierce battle that was soon to begin.

His response to our words haunts me to this day. He said, "Gentlemen, let's not be romantic." He was not being impolite, but it was his way of saying that the story of the gospel is like a romantic fairy tale—beautiful and good, but irrelevant. I believe he liked the story but didn't feel it could help him fight a war. We knew our time with a great leader had come to an end. After thanking him for the honor of meeting him, we left the palace with heavy hearts.

Early in the war with North Viet Nam another conflict surfaced in the south. It was a war of words between Diem's government and the Buddhists. The hostilities resulted in the overthrow of the Diem regime and his assassination. Duong Van Minh and other generals staged the coup on November 1, 1963. President Ngo Dinh Diem and his brother, Ngo Dinh Nhu, were murdered after their surrender the next day.

We were in the States when President Diem was killed. The bold black headlines in the paper read, "SOUTH VIET NAM'S PRESIDENT ASSASSINATED." When I read those words, my heart ached as it did in the palace when I heard him say, "Gentlemen, let's not be romantic."

I do not know what the president did when we left the palace. If he opened his heart to Christ, then we shall see him in glory someday; but if he refused to accept Christ as his personal Savior, then he is in that place of torments clearly presented in Luke 16. If he is there, I believe I know what he is thinking: "I had the opportunity to receive eternal life through faith in Christ, but I thought it was a romantic fairy tale."

CHAPTER NINE
FULL CIRCLE

The time had again arrived for furlough. I knew I should take my family back to the States for a year, but I wanted the assurance we would be permitted to return to Viet Nam. To ensure our return I secured re-entry visas.

By the time we neared the end of furlough, the war had escalated and 80 percent of the land was under curfew. The government permitted missionaries to come to Viet Nam but not to carry on a ministry that assembled large groups of people—especially in outdoor settings. I knew my ministry to Viet Nam had come to an end. We were dismayed. We loved the people, had learned their language, and had settled down to what we thought was a lifelong ministry. Our prayer to our Heavenly Commander was simple and to the point, "Now what?"

Dick Hillis had asked me to pray about directing the work in yet another field—Brazil. This would involve another culture, a different language, and a new set of challenges.

Nan and I prayed fervently about our next step but had no peace from above. The mission had rented a little home in South Bend, Indiana, for our use during furlough. It was a special treat for Nan since her parents and many other relatives lived in the area.

Bob with his pastor, Dr. H. H. Savage, 1961

I wrestled with the decision before us. In the wee hours of the morning as Nan and the children slept, a burden suddenly came to my heart. It was a burden for my home church. Dr. Savage had ministered there for thirty-eight faithful years, and I knew he was praying about retiring. The Lord was beginning to speak to me about following him. He was the only pastor I had ever had. He was pastor of the church before I was born, he was my pastor through college days, and he was still there through our ten years in the Far East.

"Follow my hero?" I thought, "that can't be! After all, I have never pastored, and the First Baptist Church of Pontiac, Michigan, with its large active membership presents a challenge too great for a thirty-two-year-old missionary." Finally from exhaustion I climbed into bed and fell asleep.

Early the next morning Nan asked, "What were you doing in the middle of the night?" I answered, "I was praying about our next move, and I feel the Lord laid a burden on my heart for Pontiac." "You mean to follow Dr. Savage as pastor of the church?" she asked. Then I said, "It really doesn't make much sense, does it?" We were both at a loss for words.

A few minutes later the phone rang. It was Dr. Savage. He said, "Bob, I couldn't sleep last night. I believe the Lord was speaking to me about you going to Pontiac to be the church's next pastor. Would you have time to come here to talk with me about it?" I responded, "I'll be right there."

A few hours later I was in the Savage living room listening as he spoke of his burden for the church and his desire that I follow him as the next undershepherd of that flock.

As the Lord would have it, Dr. Savage retired in December 1961. The following Sunday, I assumed the role of interim pastor and four months later on April 4, 1962, I became the senior pastor of my home church.

The years that followed were some of the most memorable years we have ever known. It was a special blessing being with Mom and Dad again, for they were still members of the church. It was also a time of unusual opportunities that extended further than I could have dreamed.

One day my secretary told me I had a special guest. He entered my study and introduced himself as a Christian Auca Indian. His uncle was one of the men who had killed the five young missionaries in Ecuador. He knew that our church had supported Ed McCully and wanted us to know that our interest in his people had not been in vain. He was just one of many who had trusted Christ as Savior. It was a vivid reminder that the blood of the martyr is often the seed of the church. Those young men had not died in vain. My Auca brother gave me a replica of the spear his uncle had used on that fateful day. It is in my office today as a reminder of God's grace and power.

Dr. Savage was a pioneer in radio broadcasting. We maintained and even expanded that ministry through a weekly broadcast called "Gospel Echoes." In the years that followed we had responses from listeners in thirty-six countries. Then there was the weekly television program, which God used to touch lives for Christ throughout the greater Detroit area.

Perhaps the most touching experience of our years in Pontiac came on December 5, 1967, the day I conducted the funeral of my beloved pastor. A few days before his homegoing he shared with me a poem he had written. I used it in the funeral message.

This isn't death I'm facing, but it's life forevermore.
It's not the end I'm nearing; it is ent'ring heaven's door.
The way ahead is fairer than it's ever been before,
For it's glory, yes, it's glory over yonder.

There is no fear in thinking I'll soon meet Him face to face,
The One who proved He loved me by His dying in my place.
And how I long to thank Him for His mercy and His grace,
For it's glory, yes, it's glory over yonder.

It is good to consider the past with all of its blessings, and it is fitting to consider the present with all of its challenges, but it is thrilling to consider the future with all of its joys. The past, present and future are all meaningful because of the finished work of our blessed Lord on Calvary's cross. To those who know Him as Savior, the best is yet to come.

The best is yet to come!

EPILOGUE

The purpose of this brief book has been to relate some of God's blessing upon His work in the Far East. Similar accounts could be echoed from missionaries around the world.

It seems fitting to conclude with the reminder that anything that is accomplished of eternal value results from the power of the Holy Spirit, the authority of God's Word, and the intercessory work of the Lord Jesus Christ.

God's work on earth is not finished yet. Billions are still waiting to hear the precious gospel story. Nothing would thrill the heart of this unworthy author more than to hear of some who will give of their means to the task of world evangelism as the Damers did, or respond in prayer to the needs of missionaries as Mrs. Hunt did, or to go to regions beyond as many of God's servants have done.

Perhaps some will read these words who have never opened their hearts to God's crucified and resurrected Son as Lord and Savior. If you are among that group, may I urge you to come to Christ as a penitent sinner? Believe that Jesus went to the cross with your sin upon Him and that He paid your penalty in full when He shed His blood and gave His life. Believe He arose from the dead for your justification and stands ready to save you when you open the door of your heart and invite Him to enter. At your invitation He will come into your life and you will be born into God's eternal family. God's Word is clear: "He that hath the Son hath life; and he that hath not the Son of God hath not life" (I John 5:12). This is not a romantic fairy tale—it's true!